The Spiritual Surrender Series1

5 TIPS
— *for* —
SPIRITUAL SURRENDER

*Letting Go of a False
Self - Perception*

By
Judith Anne Winters

**AWINEE
Publishing Company**

Table of Contents

Dedication 4

Foreword 5

Introduction 6

Chapter One: Tip 1 7

Chapter Two: Tip 2 10

Chapter Three: Tip 3 14

Chapter Four: Tip 4 17

Chapter Five: Tip 5 21

Afterword 24

References 25

About the Author 26

A Poem 27

Dedication

This book is dedicated, first to Spirit, the muse of my life. I am grateful for my clients who inspired me to listen and learn from their transformations. I am grateful to my family and friends who supported me with encouragement and love during the scared incubation period and finally the birth of this idea.

Foreword

You are reading this book because there is a calling in your heart for something greater in your life. You have a desire to feel happy, content, peaceful, but most of all to love yourself and others. Here you are standing at a crossroads: will you let go of things that no longer serve you. Or will you continue on the road of self- isolation, discontent, unhappiness, and most of all self-loathing and self-hate? I know, because I stood at this same juncture of my life, and I made a decision to journey forward. But I did not do it alone. I was ready to take a gigantic leap of faith into what I perceived as the unknown. I listened to Spirit, which said there is no unknown. There is only the all-loving presence of God. I asked for help, and God said, let go of people, places, and events that no longer serve you. I took a gigantic leap of faith and stopped trying to do it alone. I found my authentic self by allowing God to reign supreme in my life. There is an old saying: when the student is ready, the teacher comes. I am that teacher, guided by the Divine Spirit to share with you all that is True. You are called to your destiny right now by an all-providing, loving, and powerful desire of your soul. This is your time for spiritual surrender to that which is seeking you. It is a journey of discovery that awakens you to a higher awareness of being. You will awaken to an identity that your soul remembers. Relax and let go of rational thinking while allowing your heart to guide you.

Introduction

People often ask me what spiritual surrender is. Spiritual Surrender is the act of letting go of what no longer serves you. It is an exercise of being honest with yourself by identifying actions, events, people, and thoughts that no longer bring you peace, joy, and happiness. It is a step into an energetic frequency of action. It is a dynamic, overflowing field of unformed substance that is activated by your actions. When you let go and allow God to be the center of your life, a veil is lifted, and you see with clarity, hear minute sounds, and feel with soulful depth. To be in this state of awareness, you must allow the Presence of the Living God to speak and move through you. Your consciousness is sharpened to a height of viewing infinite possibilities surrounding you. In the next sections are five tips that have successfully assisted me and other awakening travelers in embracing their divine self through total spiritual surrender.

Chapter One

Tip 1

The question of Who I Am begins our initiation into wisdom. Most of us are taught that we are extensions of our parents. We believe that since our parents conceived us, then we must belong to or be attached to them. The opposite is true. We are God's creative idea of Itself. We came into this physical dimension as an aspect of a powerful, all seeing, universally present, and always active deity. We belong only to God/Spirit. Belonging to this deity means we have a special responsibility to love ourselves, love the divine, and to love others. Loving ourselves is a sacred act. It involves recognizing our unique individualized expression as the ONE. We have a sacred duty to begin by loving our authentic selves as we evolve.

What is authenticity? Merriam-Webster defines authenticity as "true to one's spirit or character." What causes an individual to be authentic? Loving! Loving of oneself and loving God and all life forms. It is our divine nature to express from this higher vibration of love. When we "move against the grain," so to speak, this causes a disharmony within our body temple which cascades outward into the world. I remember when, at the age of around 45, I wanted to be married again. My husband of five years died when I was 37. I felt desperate, believing that I needed to have a companion in my life. From this inner belief, I went looking for a mate. Well, you know the result: I entwined myself with a man who did not want to be married again. I thought that, if I loved him enough, he would change his mind. WRONG. WRONG. WRONG. Wrong thinking and erroneous results. What I was living from was a belief that I would be happy when married to him. During a midnight crisis, I asked myself, who am I? Through the pain, I recognized that I did not love myself. I did not know who I was. Subconsciously, I wanted to be like my mother and all the women I watched while growing up in the deep South, in a segregated community. Single women were not honored, respected, or considered a whole person during that era unless they were married. I observed that they were made to feel less than their married sisters, aunts, and cousins.

My false perceptions, though, were a blessing because they led me on an inward journey, a quest to find my True identity. This identity was not about a physical egocentric presence; instead, my personality sought to connect with the divine nature of my being. To begin, I learned to give up and let go of beliefs that no longer served my living a life of Self-Love and Joy. My reflection in the mirror showed me a beautiful, loving, and intelligent woman who loved God. My journey has been extended and deepened because, as I released from my mind beliefs, feelings and behavior which were not channeled by ego, I learned the true meaning of Self-Love. This is not a romantic idealism nor is it a feeling to escape from reality. Instead, loving is the action of being in a state of awareness where ego serves a purpose, but it is not in charge of my life. Loving is the activity of living from my heart-wisdom which is the center of my soul. I changed my beliefs about who I am because I wanted to love from my heart. My point of view focused on me, not on the opinions about me from my family, friends, or the world. I became a living, walking, loving energy field of gratitude.

I feel that you are ready to do the same because you are reading this book. I encourage you to stop here and practice the exercises in the Workbook Chapter 1. They are designed to inspire and gently nudge you onto the path to loving yourself.

Chapter Two

Tip 2

The new science teaches that everything in the universe arose from unformed substance. In the creation mythology, the Living Presence declared, let there be Light, and so it was. From this energetic field, we are created in the image and likeness of the Creator: God and we are named Good. We have the same power as the Creator to declare something, and it will manifest according to our conviction. The old science declared that matter was separate from everything. We accepted that everything happens in a linear sequence, such as A equals B equals C. The new science teaches that the Universe is made of an unformed substance called energy, which is never destroyed. It changes form. If everything is an energetic field, then physical forms manifest according to the observer making an observation. The observer and the observed are one. There is no separation. The universe is always friendly because it is affected by our desires and wishes. We create what appears to be an unstable universe due to our thinking. When we totally surrender to Spirit and declare, Yes, I am ready to serve by loving, this causes a transformation in our energetic field. We create our reality.

Albert Einstein discovered that matter/mass and energy are one, as indicated by the formula $E = mc2$. The PBS television program, NOVA, dramatizes the remarkable story behind this equation in "Einstein's Big Idea" (PBS). How does loving and serving others affect an energetic field? Loving and serving are active energy fields which begin with your beliefs and the ideas that hold your attention. The focus we give to someone or something becomes a mirror reflection of our views. Thoughts of joy reflect a dynamic feeling that life is good. Similarly, thoughts of lack, limitation, and worry reflect feelings of conflict and disharmony, materializing in our daily lives. Thus, what you think about becomes a physical form.

Liz is a single young woman who wanted to overcome her anxious feelings when in the presence of male friends. Liz described herself as outgoing, someone who found it easy to meet people and make friends; she was a financially independent with a passion for good food, travel, and yoga. She expressed a desire to meet someone to share her life. When asked about her primary goal, she said, "I want to feel less anxious about meeting this person. I want a better life." Liz expressed two paradigms: first, a realization she could feel less worried, and, second, a recognition that her life could be better.

Over the span of several meetings, Liz changed her wants into action by recognizing unhealthy habits of feeling. She realized that she reacted to the presence of males in her company with flight and fright responses. In her body, she felt sensations of energy but was unaware of their origin. She wanted to raise her awareness and her understanding of the meaning of these feelings. Whenever she felt a crisis coming, Liz listened to her body, thereby, gradually changing her thoughts and noticing a change in her energy levels. Liz had felt lethargic, unable to focus when feeling anxious. But she soon started to see that her beliefs about meeting men began in childhood when she was coached by her mother that she was not safe around men unless she knew them. Gradually she changed this narrative through meditation, prayer, yoga, and experimentation. Moreover, she sought the comfort of being with friends as she explored conversing with men she did not know. Liz slowly developed healthy feeling habits towards men she met outside of her comfort zone, leading her deeper in the practice of yoga which resulted in an expanding awareness of feeling energy everywhere. She no longer held false beliefs because she changed her perception about life.

Penny Pierce is a clairvoyant empath and intuition trainer who writes that "We come into the world with a personal vibration and we allow this energy to bring us to our home frequency. Home frequency is the vibration of your soul as it expresses through your body" (Pierce, 100).

We are born with this frequency, and it is our responsibility to know and feel it in our daily life adventure. We receive valuable information through the body's temple as we navigate our way through our life's activities. However, if we hold on to difficult situations, people, and events which can be labeled as negative, the flow of energy becomes bundled and tightened like wires on a pipe line. The flow stops, and we feel its effect through the body as dis-ease. Perhaps the greatest mystery of our being is accepting that we are spiritual beings with a body, not a body with a spiritual essence. We are the I AM that I AM that is known by the ancient mystics and written in the sacred texts. Our mission is to glorify Spirit in all the ways of living. Each individual life form has a purpose, and the home frequency shows us a glimpse of this purpose. However, it is our choice to accept and to follow it.

Marc is another example of leaning into the I AM energy of self-acceptance. He attends a school of theology with a goal of becoming a traveling minister. In prayer class, he volunteers to begin the class with meditation, a style that includes drumming and singing. Not only is this way of prayer accepted by his classmates and instructors, but everyone tells him that it brings peace and joy to their souls. However, following one particular prayer, the instructor chastised him for not following her rules for praying in this class. Marc felt like a child being scolded for something that was not clear to him. Yet he remembered what he learned during our time together: everything is energy. When confronted with negative energy, call on the I AM presence as what you are: an energetic force that has the capacity to dissolve what is not accepted. He stood his ground and chanted silently to himself, "Right now I AM Love." He repeated I AM LOVE until he felt the energy embrace her as she walked away. Love energy became the catalyst that caused the instructor to recall that she had not explained her policy. Then, when he asked, "Are we okay now," she responded, "Yes, we are okay." Marc stood in a personal vibration and home frequency of Love.

Are you ready to accept and experience the power of home frequency? Now it is time to open the Workbook Chapter 2 and practice your experience of energy.

Chapter Three

Tip 3

Stillness and silence are powerful tools we embrace in our daily spiritual practice. Stillness is the absence of physical movement. The most powerful form of stillness is meditation. Allowing the mind to give full attention to the Omnipresence of God brings a full recognition of our connection with Spirit. In this powerful state of awareness, we Listen. We Listen with an inner ear that is both sacred and sacramental. In this heightened state of awareness, the Living Presence speaks to us in a single word or words, pictures, and music.

Courage gives us wings to fly. Audacity allows you to trust your heart. Being still and listening are paths to courage, for they require you to commit to a non-movement of the body for some needed time. Stillness and listening are features of our genetic inheritance. We are born to follow our intuition. However, often we bypass it with thoughts of lack, limitation, and worry. I graduated from an adult high school because I dropped out of regular high school in my senior year due to complications in my family. I felt lack, limitation, and doubt as I tried to live my life as an adult. My attention focused on returning to school for a high school diploma. I sat for hours, dreaming of how my life would change. I enrolled in an adult high school program where a classmate invited me to attend a meditation group. During the 1960s, transcendental meditation was popular. I learned to meditate and felt the peace I desired. I meditated day and night while I completed my senior year of high school. I sat on a cushion and sometimes on the floor as I breathed slowly in and out, focusing on my breath. Relaxation came swiftly because my breath reminded me of the feeling I experience when jogging. I remember seeing a soft light flooding the center of my forehead with my eyes closed. As I gently slowed my breathing, I heard a small voice say, "You are my beloved. All is well." Tears flowed freely down my cheeks. I felt a sense of peace and love. I knew instantly that this meditation thing was for me. From the first time I meditated, I continue this process wherever I am. I welcome contemplation in silence, around people, while walking, while visiting in the forest, and anytime I behold the surrounding beauty of nature. Stillness and silence are my mascots for living a spiritual life.

Some perspectives hold that "real" meditation happens when the body is still. Stillness is useful when one is learning to meditate, for it allows the mind to rest. However, once you have found your meditation center, contemplation may happen wherever you are.

Robert, a psychiatric nurse, works in the psychiatric ward of a general hospital. He described his work hours as chaotic and stressful. He worked a twelve- hour shift five days of the week. Every other Saturday, he worked eight hours. Robert wanted to learn how to meditate, but could not find the time to learn on his own. He said that slouching on the couch in front of the television, then falling asleep in his clothes were his methods of relaxing. His long hours at the hospital did not allow him time to eat a good meal and experience periods of restful sleep before returning to work. Robert said, "I want to relax. I don't know how to do this."

My work with Robert began with identifying his beliefs about work. His work habits formed when he worked as a writer during his teen years. His father reminded him that hard work was the key to success. After further exploration, Robert realized that his work schedule contributed to increased stress in his body and mind. He loved his job but wanted to manage the stress and begin to socialize with his friends. He read in a magazine that meditation would help him achieve his desires of a lifestyle change. During the initial stages of learning to sit in silence, he selected the affirmation "Today I am relaxing" and included it in his mediation time. Although this technique is slightly different from the traditional model of stillness and listening, I thought it best for him to focus his attention on something that he desired. Then, at some point in his process, Robert would know when to let go of the mantra. Gradually, he reported that he felt comfortable in the stillness and silence and that he learned to relax.

Are you ready to listen while sitting in stillness and silence? I invite you to open the Workbook to Chapter 3 and begin.

Chapter Four

Tip 4

Psychology teaches that intuition is a something we all possess, but only a few of us give it our full attention. Intuition is perceived as a hunch; an idea; a clarity that causes us to ask, am I really hearing this? To answer this question, we must go beyond our sense perception. We must feel comfortable in the invisible world, alert in our dream world; we must love the unknown, or the spaces in between. Intuition is that place in consciousness where we intuitively know something or feel something. Some call it a hunch; or a lightning swift word or message in the gut. Trusting the message is key to powerful Spiritual surrender. Trusting means letting go of socialized beliefs about what is real. Most often we think of real as what we see in the physical form. As discussed in Chapter 2, real is what we feel as this energetic field of unformed substance. Hence, the message comes from the deepest part of our being; our soul. Is this a physical place? No; again, it is a feeling space that transcends words. When we trust the message we are saying YES, I am available, ready to step into my highest good. We receive and feel an energy in the body when we say YES. Energy embodies every organ, cell, and atom of the body. It holds the remembrance of all events, small or large, remarkable or unremarkable. A litmus test for feeling our inward disposition can be noticed (if we pay attention) in this humble form. Social scientists have found that the heart is the center of emotional intelligence and not the brain (Heart Math Research).

Our heart is the center of knowing, awareness; and insight for enlightenment. Developmental Biologists support the idea that it is the first organ to form in the embryo. We are feeling beings from the beginning of creation. If the body is the receiver of our emotions, then we notice its response to every thought, word, and action. One day, while I sat in meditation, the still small voice said, 'A hobby of your choice.' My response was "Walking is my hobby." Then I heard, "Walk in competition." I listened, then obeyed. In past years, I have admired the competitive spirit of female competitive runners. I respected women who competed in the track and field competitions. I felt a longing in my heart to do something outside of my physical fitness comfort zone. The message I received was timely and confirmed my next adventure. I joined a race walking club with the intention of mastering this sport and then competing in the Los Angeles Marathon. My heart said yes. My body tingled with excitement as I declared an intention to race walk in the next marathon. By trusting the message and following heart- wisdom, my self-confidence increased dramatically.

The race walk club trained me in the skills of competitive race walking. During training days, I heard Spirit's message that became a beacon of light which I followed, thereby feeling deep gratitude and love. I finished the race within five hours. I received a medal, and my soul rejoiced at this accomplishment.

Do you have a heartfelt desire to serve more in your life? Perhaps your heart is telling you to step away from the job and do it. Heart warnings can come in the form of an urging to be something greater, a voice that says you can do it, or a longing for a desire. If there is a heart longing, then it is Spirit speaking to you. In a later chapter, I speak about heart coherence. Alignment with the Divine begins with the heart resonating in a fluid flow of love as what you are. There is no separation between you and the Divine.

Pamela dreamed often of writing a novel, an essay, an article. Her dreams came in the form of pens writing on paper. Sometimes, her hand was behind the pen. Other times, she was a witness to her accepting an award for writing a novel. She talked about the stories in her head and how they wanted to escape onto paper. Our work began with identifying whether she believed that she could write for people to read and feel inspired. However, her beliefs were inconsistent with her desire. In meditation, she experienced the vision, but she failed to act on it. She did not trust the message given to her. The blockage came when, in college, she was told to write an essay about anything. She chose to write about her early life living in the deep South. The instructor graded her down and told her she could not write. Pamela felt devastated by these remarks. She held this belief as a truth about herself. Consequently, her desire and the belief were in contrast and did not support her longing. Her internal work was to gradually erase the old belief and replace it with thoughts that she was capable and, more importantly, that writing was her purpose. First, Pamela learned to recognize and accept who and what she is. Prayer, meditation, and the creation of affirmative statements to guide her became tools for letting go and letting God be the messenger in her life. Life Visioning became a primary technique which assisted her to know that God's highest vision for her was to be a writer. She listened, trusted the message, and obeyed the call. She dissolved the barriers that prevented her movement. Today, Pamela is a best-selling author of spiritually inspiring books. She worked consistently to remove the internal negative beliefs which kept her from materializing her dreams. In doing so, she freed herself from the bondage of "I am not good enough; I cannot do it," which someone had inflicted on her. Do you listen to internal and external messages that do not resonate with your desires? Let them go NOW! Allow the Presence of the Living God to work through you. Listen, then obey.

I encourage you to listen to the still voice within as it guides you to activities beyond your wildest imagination. Now is the time to open the Workbook Chapter 4 where you will find practice exercises to help you on your way to trusting the message.

Chapter Five

Tip 5

Saying Yes, I am ready to express my love in the world, is a sacred action of love. True love is generosity and kindness towards ourselves and all of God's creation. True love is loving when it is hard to love; loving beyond forgiveness. Loving is not a romantic expression. It is a way to bring forth a goodness in everyone and everything. It is the love that the earlier prophet taught his disciples and followers. To Love others as much as you love yourself. But loving yourself comes first, because without self-love, we do not love God, nor do we love one another. Welcome home to the joy of feeling the flow of love! It is the whipped cream and cherry on top of your favorite dessert. It is the uncertainty with excitement. You don't need to search for loving adventures outside of yourself. You already have IT! Do you know that we came into the world with Loving DNA molecules? They transmit signals to the body when we are in a state of giving or receiving love. When was the last time you felt love? When was the last time you gave it away without any expectations? Did you send love vibrations to someone today? Did you receive love vibrations from someone or something today? Loving is an essential quality of our lives. To love and be loved are actionable events. There are feelings of contentment, joy, harmony, and peace within our soul. We are born to love! We represent the essence of love. We are love in action. There is no escaping this feeling of magic and grandiosity. Our bodies become the radar for signaling whether we are open to loving or denying the action of loving. The electromagnetic field which surrounds us is like a beacon emitting waves of energy. There is no separation between our actions and body mass. Together, they are an energetic force which signals the mind when it is time to let go and be open to loving.

Angelica dreamed of a better life, but she did not know how it would materialize. She focused on wanting a home and a better job. It happened that all three desires materialized. She felt a stirring in her heart saying that there was more for her to be. Angelica used willpower to make things happen. However, while willpower gets you moving, it may also lead to feelings of exhaustion. She wanted to experience peace, harmony, and love. She reached a crossroads of two basic choices: to feel a flow of expanding self-awareness or to feel afraid and dismiss the flowing energy within her soul. She sought my help to connect with the flow of self-love and eventually the actions of loving others. Her situation is not unique because we often feel the energetic flow in the body, but fail to stop, acknowledge it, and then seek to know the insight. The spiritual tools of meditation, affirmative prayer, insight, and self-love apply in this case. She focused on all the processes described in the previous chapters, letting go of beliefs that no longer benefited her and allowing her to identify the divine purpose in your life. In this case, Angelica listened to the still small voice which gave her the courage to go deeper into her soul and accept her spiritual identity. With the courage to disallow outside influences to guide her life, she disciplined her body and mind to focus on God's love and grace. She followed her heart-wisdom and started a successful Internet business.

A final thought: gratitude is the powerful red satin bow that rests within the divine package of our humanity. There is no simpler prayer than to say "I AM Grateful." There is a feeling of magic when those three words are spoken. They are a swirling energetic frequency which quenches the hunger for spiritual food and brings peace to those who are speechless when experiencing a miracle. Whatever the situation, when we pray thankfulness, the Light encircles the multiverse. It brings all nature to its knees in adoration of our divine gifts. We are created with Grace to stand tall, upright, and dignified as we proclaim the glory of God. In this elegant and sacred space, no one feels alone because we are home. Despite the trials and tribulations which happen in one's physical lifetime, gratitude always brings us home to our unique and authentic selves. However, we must let go of belief, thoughts, feelings that no longer bring us to a higher good. Thankfulness and unthankfulness do not exist in the same field. Heart coherence must exist within the heart-mind-body in order to materialize our desires. There exists a synergy of love which pours into the mold of creation. In this space of loving, we occupy rooms in our home for devotional caring; loving self and God; feeling the I AM of our being; listening to the small voice; trusting Intuition; and always loving. Who we are and what we are is eternal, imperishable; thus, there is no hurry for the next event or ritual. We have it all now. We are here; we are now; we are IT. Gratitude is the bond that holds together the forms we create.

You are ready to step into your greatness of loving self, loving God and loving all life forms. Today is the time to open your Workbook Chapter 5 and begin the practice exercises.

Afterword

Now that you have successfully applied the Five Tips for Spiritual Surrender to your knowledge base, it is time to begin embodying these tips into your daily practice. You may begin by keeping a journal that describes your daily feelings and thoughts. These entries give you a picture of what you are experiencing inside. Transformation is an inside job. It does not happen in the physical world. As you awaken to your true identity, the magic begins. Series 2 continues with further defining the transformational process. This series offers exercises that assist you along the way.

References

1. HeartMath. Science of the Heart: Exploring the Role of the Heart in Human Performance. Retrieved June 11, 2018 from http://www.heartmath.org/research/science-of-the-heart-brain-communication

2. PBS NOVA (2005, October 11). Einstein's Big Ideas. Retrieved June 1, 2018 from http://www.pbs.org/wgbh/nove/physics/einstein-big-ideas-html

3. Pierce, Penny (2009). Frequency. (New York: Simon & Schuster/ Hillsboro: Oregon: Beyond Words).

About the Author

Rev. Dr. Judith Anne Winters is an ordained minister, Doctorate of Divinity, and Agape Licensed Spiritual Counselor. She is a master seminar leader, master alchemist, and master of transmutation. She is founder and Spiritual Director of Spirit of the Earth Ministry. Rev. Judith shares her gifts with the world as a Spiritual Intuitive and Transformational Life Coach.

Ode to the Creator

Light breaks the dawn
A gentle swirl of air envelops the space
Silence is the stillness of the moment
Whispers gently brush the treetops
As raindrops gently fall slowly to the ground
Rainbow colors permeate the sky
Awe and wonder dance like twins
When darkness births a new beginning.
It is Good; Very Good.

Redhawk, 1985

www.ingramcontent.com/pod-product-compliance
Lightning Source LLC
Chambersburg PA
CBHW070050040426
42331CB00034B/2983